Professor Birdsong's

157
DUMBEST THIEVES

Thieves, Thugs & Rogues Series: Book One

Leonard Birdsong
Winghurst Publications

Professor Birdsong's Dumbest: Thieves, Thugs, and Rogues by Leonard Birdsong
© 2020 Leonard Birdsong
All rights reserved.
Printed in the USA.

ISBN: 978-0-9979573-2-7 (Kindle)
ISBN: 978-0-9979573-3-4 (Paperback)

Winghurst Publications
1969 S. Alafaya Trail / Suite 303
Orlando,   FL   32828-8732
www.BirdsongsLaw.com
lbirdsong22@gmail.com

Disclaimer:

Permissions:

Cover graphics: ©Khalid S. Birdsong /
http:friedchickenandsushi.com

Book cover design: Rik Feeney /
www.RickFeeney.com

Acknowledgments

I wish to acknowledge Rik Feeney who has been my stalwart book consultant who has made my dreams of being a Humor author come true.

I also wish to acknowledge my son Khalid Birdsong for the cover art he has done for me over the years. He has been paid handsomely.

Professor Birdsong's 157 Dumbest Thieves

Table of Contents

Introduction

Law Professor Leonard Birdsong lives in Florida where he has taught Criminal Law, Evidence, and Immigration Law. He has written many scholarly legal pieces since joining the legal academy. This is not one of those scholarly pieces!

This trilogy series of Professor Birdsong's newest *Dumbest Criminal Stories: Thieves, Thugs & Rogues* is written just for fun and enjoyment. It showcases stories from all over the world and contains the k i n d of m a n y d u m b , funny and weird criminal law stories that he has found and written about since 2008. Read them. Laugh at the stories and then go to Amazon.com and choose from his other inexpensive fourteen humor books for more such laughs.

Professor Birdsong's 157 Dumbest Thieves

Preface

157 Dumbest Thieves

This first book of the trilogy, *Thieves, Thugs, and Rogues* is devoted to thieves. As you already know the word thieves is the plural of the word thief. A thief is defined as a person who steals another's property, especially by stealth and without using force or violence. The origins of the word thief as we know it today comes from the old English word "thiof" which meant one who steals. The Old English word is close in origin to the Dutch word "dief" which means one who steals, as well as the German word "dieb," which also means to steal.

In today's America the word robber and thief are often used interchangeably. The real difference at law between the two is that robbery is mainly accomplished by force or threat of force.

Just about everyone in the world learns the meaning of theft before they enter kindergarten. Now with this knowledge feast your eyes on these newest stories of dumb thieves and get your laugh on.

Professor Birdsong's 157 Dumbest Thieves

CHAPTER 1

Thieves from Way Down East

We start with a few stories of Dumbest thieves from the New England area and one from the district of Columbia. What a good place to start.

Enjoy!

Professor Birdsong's 157 Dumbest Thieves

CONNECTICUT: *"Dyeing to land in jail," read the headline.* It has been reported that a serial bank robber who didn't wear a disguise when he robbed three banks and paid for a motel room with dye-soaked bills has been sentenced to 10 years in prison. A judge told Andre Edwards, 41, in January 2019, "you were not very clever," pointing out that the Hamden man did nothing to conceal his identity during the robberies and was "all over the surveillance tapes," then paid for a room with money covered in red dye. His public defender said Edwards has a substance abuse problem.

CONNECTICUT: *Could he have ripped off the wrong fellow.* We learn that in January of 2018 a man stole a rookie police officer's personal vehicle and went on a buying spree with the victim's credit cards at Taco Bell and Walmart. Derrick Johnson, 21, stole the car in Waterbury on January 23, the night of the officer's Police Academy graduation. He was caught in March and was charged with burglary, second degree larceny and identity theft.

CONNECTICUT: *Justice delayed...is justice denied.* A descendant of 19th century Supreme Court Justice Roger B. Taney overruled the late jurist and apologized for his kin's infamous ruling in the *Dred Scott* case. Charles Taney IV of Greenwich, apologized to St. Louis resident Lynne Jackson, a great-great-granddaughter of Scott, a freed slave who famously sought voting rights after his owner, who had freed him, took him to a free state. The apology came in March 2017, on the 160-year anniversary of Dred Scott v. Sandford. Scott had filed a petition seeking to vote in the free state. Justice Taney wrote for the 7-2 majority, saying that only citizens of the U.S. could vote and that a person of African descent could never be a citizen of the United States. Scotts' bid to vote failed.

CONNECTICUT: *Disbarred!* In mid-January 2019, a judge accepted former Trump campaign manager Paul Manafort's proposal to permanently give up his right to practice law in the state amid disbarment proceedings. Judge David Sheridan also issued a finding of misconduct related to Manafort's guilty pleas in special counsel Robert Mueller's investigation of Russian interference in the 2016 presidential election. Manafort a New Britain native was admitted to the Connecticut bar in 1974. His right to practice law in the District of Columbia also had been recently suspended.

MAINE: *Bank robbery slipup...* A bank robbery suspect slipped up while making a getaway. Jason Mackenrodt, 38, robbed the Bangor Savings Bank, then ran across four lanes of traffic and a restaurant parking lot before he slipped on a patch of ice, police report. A police officer saw Mackenrodt drop cash and a pistol as he fell, helped him up and arrested him.

MASSACHUSETTS: *The headline read, "Caught dead-handed."* The so-called "Obit Bandit," is a man who had been accused of breaking into homes while residents attended wakes and funerals. He recently pleaded not guilty to burglary and larceny charges. Randy Brunelle, 35, was held in lieu of $25,000 bail. Police believe he is responsible for three break-ins on Cape Cod while Plymouth police suspect him in five similar break-ins. His current arrest came in February after allegedly breaking-into a Barnstable woman's home while she was at her mother's wake.

MASSACHUSETTS: *Amnesia, maybe?* It has been reported that police did not have to look very far to find a sleepy suspect wanted in a knifepoint holdup in the town of Pittsfield. Melissa Holden, 40, allegedly used a knife to steal two pints of vodka and a bottle of Gatorade from a liquor store – and then passed out in a nearby building where police arrested her. Her attorney says she has no memory of the crime.

MASSACHUSETTS: *Police solve case of "fowl" play.* Police officer Wayne Thornhill of the Seekonk police department recently pulled over a car and saw a backpack in the backseat move on its own. The backpack turned out to be stuffed with seven chickens stolen from a nearby farm. The 20-year-old driver was arrested for larceny and animal cruelty. We learn, further, that the chickens were returned to their owner.

VERMONT: *The headline read, "Getaway diver."* A robber on the run from police tried to make a getaway by driving into a lake. Police encountered the man while searching for a suspect in an armed robbery of a gas station. The store clerk saw the suspect was wearing an ankle monitor and police traced him to a car travelling through the town of Berkshire. After a 20-mile car chase the suspect drove onto a dock and straight into St Albans Bay. He got out of the car and tried to swim away before Officers caught him on an adjacent dock. We learn that the unidentified man is facing several charges.

WASHINGTON D.C.: *The headline read, "He could have used better intelligence."* A Jamaican man chose the wrong man to scam when he tried to flimflam William Webster – the only man in history to have led both the CIA and the FBI. Now he has been convicted and sent to prison for six years. Keniel Thomas kept threatening the former top spy and G-man, authorities said, so Webster's wife got some of her husband's former colleagues on a conference call one day when Thomas phoned to demand money. He later pled guilty to extortion. His previous scams had allegedly earned him $300,000.

Professor Birdsong's 157 Dumbest Thieves

CHAPTER 2

New York, New Jersey & Pennsylvania Thieves

Professor Birdsong's 157 Dumbest Thieves

NEW YORK CITY: *The shampoo thief and the tour bus.*
A drunken dandruff-shampoo thief dashed out of a drug
store near times Square one Friday afternoon in January
2018 – and ran smack into a tour bus, breaking his leg and
at least one of the plastic bottles of stolen shampoo. The
unidentified man wound up splayed out on the pavement
on 47th Street at Eighth Avenue, along with nine $8.95
bottles of Head & Shoulders Old Spice Swagger Shampoo
for men. He was placed on a gurney and taken to Bellvue
Hospital, said a police source who descried the man as
39-years old, homeless, emotionally disturbed and "highly
intoxicated."

NEW YORK: *Panty raiding Judge?* A Long Island judge
accused of snatching a pair of his neighbor's dirty panties
was suspended by the state in April of 2018. Suffolk
County District Judge Robert Cicale, 49, was put on paid
leave after his arrest. The facts of the case reveal that
Cicale's 23-year-old East Islip neighbor was home alone
on a Thursday when she heard a noise and saw a man
matching the judge's description un off. Cicale was later
found carrying multiple "soiled female undergarments.
He was formerly charged with second-degree burglary.

NEW JERSEY: *He dropped in and couldn't climb out!* Benny Ramirez, 30, allegedly cut a hole in a roof, raided a pizzeria cash register but had no way to get out, Hoboken police said. He then broke his way into the liquor store next door, got drunk and passed out, according to the arresting officers.

NEW YORK: *"The sicko was not slick-o,"* read the *headline.* We learn that a pervert hid a cellphone in the ladies' room of a Long Island office building to record women using the facilities – but also captured his face on the video leading police right to him in January 2019. Daniel Perez, 20, allegedly slipped into the women's bathroom of an office building in Great neck, secreted the phone away and hit record, according to police. A horrified woman later discovered the phone and turned it over to police detectives who used the accidental evidence to track Perez to his home where he was arrested and charged with three counts of unlawful surveillance.

NEW JERSEY: *"Flush with patriotism,"* read the *headline.* We learn that a man has filed suit after his town prosecuted him for displaying three toilets and confederate flags in his front yard. Michael Speece displayed the toilets – one white, one red, and one blue, outside his home along with other decorations including the flags. Speece maintains that the town of Winslow, 15 miles southeast of Philadelphia, violated his rights of free speech and free use of his property. His suit seeks unspecified damages and expenses.

NEW JERSEY: *$1,500 belt swiped and found!* A passenger at Newark Airport in early January 2018, took off his $1,500 Louis Vuitton belt for a security screening and it was allegedly stolen by a janitor, according to Port Authority police. The New Jersey man, 28, took off his belt when he went through security around 8 pm, but couldn't find it at the other end, so he reported it stolen. Police scanned security footage and saw airport cleaner Osmal Reyes, 43, allegedly in possession of the belt. We learn that Reyes faces a charge of theft after police confronted him and found the belt rolled up in a side pocket of his work trolley.

NEW JERSEY: *The headline read, "Wait a minute, wait a minute, Mr. Postman."* Leonard Gresham, a former, Newark mailman, plead guilty in early February to taking nearly $15,000 in bribes to deliver packages containing illegal drugs. Gresham, 50, admitted intercepting and personally dropping off the parcels, authorities said.

PENNSYLVANIA: *This "Stiff" has been stiffing the state.* It has been reported that Jarrett Stiff is the Keystone State's worst toll evader, and now he is being forced to pay up. The 36-year-old from Philly had racked up fines totaling $128,000 in unpaid tolls and fines barreling through the cashless toll lanes on the Pennsylvania Turnpike between 2012 and 2017 and ignoring bills after cameras recorded his license plate.

PENNSYLVANIA: *Instead of trying to break out of a police station she broke in a station house.* Ashley Keister, 27, was caught on surveillance camera using a large cigarette butt receptacle to smash the glass doors of the West Wyoming Police Department on a Monday morning in early January 2019. It appears that Ms. Keister was looking for an officer she had been hounding romantically since he arrested her last May for violation of an order of protection obtained by her former domestic partner, police said.

PENNSLVANIA: *The headline read, "They were dopey rollers.* An overweight husband and wife duo allegedly stole a purse from a Walmart shopper and sped away on motorized scooters provided by the store. Robert Doerwald, 54, and Dawn Hosie, 45, were caught on camera snatching a customer's purse at the store in the town of Honesdale and rolling away. Police report that they later surrendered.

PENNSYLVANIA: *Large "scale" drug bust?* Police raided a home in Chester County and found heroin, fentanyl and wads of cash along with a three-foot alligator living in the kitchen. Irvin Hawkins, Aki Gathright, and Tyrone Jackson were charged with drug offenses.

PENNSYLVANIA: *Hip Hop, maybe?* Police in the town of Bedminster arrested Loren McCutcheon, 52, for allegedly trying to steal a kangaroo from a petting zoo. She was stopped trying to load the Peaceable Kingdom kangaroo named Jeffrey into her Honda Pilot. She claimed Jeffrey belonged to her and she was taking him home to Florida, police said.

PENNSYLVANIA: *This teacher needs to learn a few lessons.* Tara Smith, a Susquentia High School mathematics teacher, not only stole a white Coach bag, wallet, $250 in cash and a Victoria's Secret gift card from a student, police say that Ms. Smith, 32, was silly enough to use the gift card herself to buy items she had shipped to her own home, according to the police who arrested her for grand theft.

PENNSYLVANIA: *Liar, liar, panties on fire.* A former state beauty queen who faked having leukemia to benefit from fund-raisers has been sentenced to two to four years in prison. A judge in Bellefonte sentenced Brandi Weaver, 24. She pleaded guilty in July 2016. Investigators believe that she conned at least 165 people into donating $30,000 to her fraudulent scheme.

PENNSYLVANIA: *Brainiac?* A man stole a human brain from a science lab and used it to get high. Joshua long, 26, of Carlisle, allegedly dipped his marijuana in the formaldehyde used to preserve the brain and then stashed the brain under his porch. A frightened relative called police when she found the brain wrapped in a shopping bag under the porch. Of course, you know that dipping marijuana into formaldehyde turns the weed into what is known as "angel dust."

PENNSYLVANIA: The headline read: "Gal's bra a 3G cup: cops. A supervisor at Sands Casino Resort in Bethlehem tried to steal $3,000 worth of chips from a craps table by hiding them in her bra. Brandy Cheatham, 44, admitted to hiding $500 chips in her bra while in a casino elevator, authorities say. She could not be reached for further comment for this report.

CHAPTER 3

Thieves from Down South

Professor Birdsong's 157 Dumbest Thieves

ALABAMA: *Hide the car keys from this kid.* A 12—year-old Alabama boy was so mad with his parents that he swiped his mother's car and drove it 75 miles across state lines. The wannabe juvenile delinquent made all the way to New Augusta, Mississippi, where he stopped for gas. That was the end of the line for him because a worker at the gas station worker called police to report the pint-sized joyrider car thief.

GEORGIA: *It's my home now!* We learn that a family recently came home from vacation to find someone else living in their house. Janice Henson said the key wouldn't turn when she and her family returned to their Marietta home on a Wednesday in early January 2019. Then 26-year-old Nathaniel Nuckols of Canton came to the door, told her to leave and said it was his home now, she told police. Nucklos allegedly threatened to shoot police and was arrested after a five hour stand off with Cobb County police. The home's locks had been changed, drawers emptied, family photos moved, and all the food was gone, Ms. Henson said. Nucklos was arrested and charged with burglary and making terrorist threats.

LOUISIANA: *Concealed weapon?* A man was caught hiding a gun between his buttocks at a police station police, report. Justin Savoie had been arrested for possession of marijuana and a homemade gun when police performed strip-search while booking him, said Golden Meadow Police, adding they found a small pistol in his rump.

LOUSIANA: *A burglar caught orange-handed!* A Monroe, homeowner entered her residence in mid-April 2018 to discover a naked woman in her bathtub, chomping on Cheetos while taking a bath. The suspect, Evelyn Washington, 29, was arrested on burglary and property damage charges. There was no charge for eating Cheetos while bathing.

NORTH CAROLINA: *IDIOT!* We learn that a teenage crook robbed a 9-year-old's organic lemonade stand – jabbing a gun into the boy's stomach and demanding cash. The young boy had been selling lemonade to raise money for his lawn mowing business in the town of Monroe when the bandit struck. The idiot made off with $13, which police later found stashed in nearby woods

NORTH CAROLINA: *Free Keg party?* It has been reported that a brewery offered a free keg party to anyone who found its stolen delivery van –and got extra-quick results. The Charlotte-based Unknown Brewing Company announced the reward with a photo of the missing van on Facebook. Forty-two minutes later, a woman named Caroline called to say she saw the vehicle on her block – "a new record for finding a stolen van," the brewery reported.

NORTH CAROLINA: *Irony?* It has been reported that good Samaritans stopped to help a man get his truck out of a ditch. However, it turned out that they did a big favor for themselves. How so? They noticed in the truck items that had earlier been stolen from the auto parts store where they all worked. They called the police and the 27-year-old suspect was arrested.

NORTH CAROLINA: *"Bad move!" reads the headline.* A would-be kidnapper chased a woman into a karate studio and was pummeled into submission by a black belt instructor, police report. The woman broke free and ran for help at Bushiken Karate Charlotte Dojo, where Randall Ephraim was tidying up the place. He unleashed a beat down, landing the suspect in the hospital.

NORTH CAROLINA: *Jesus calls 911?* In mid-March Richard Quintero, 46, allegedly broke into a High Point Pizza Hut and stuffed his face with several slices of pizza and Mountain Dew. He then called 911 and claimed to be the son of God. "Yes, this is Jesus Christ and I just broke into the Pizza Hut." Quintero reportedly said. "Jesus is here now. He's back to earth." Police quickly arrived and arrest him for burglary.

SOUTH CAROLINA: *Fake dough for doughnuts?* Police say that a man used a fake $100 bill in an effort to buy pastries at a doughnut ship in Myrtle Beach. He went through the drive-thru and handed the cashier a bill bearing the disclaimer: "For motion picture use only." When the man was challenged, he fled the scene – without doughnuts

SOUTH CAROLINA: *Only half-naked?* In mid-February 2019, a half-naked woman sprinted onto a runway at an airport, sparking chaos and delaying flights. The unnamed traveler peeled off down to her undies at Florence Regional Airport and ran across the Tarmac until police corralled her.

SOUTH CAROLINA: *The headline read, "Shave and a hair-caught."* We learn that three civilian workers have been convicted in a scheme to sell $1.5 million worth of shaving supplies stolen from a Marine Corps store. Orlando Byson, Tommie Harrison, Jr., and Sarah Brutus pleaded guilty in late- January 2019, in Charleston to conspiracy to defraud the U.S., and face five years in prison. They admitted they worked with a noncommissioned Marine Corps officer to sell the razors and razor blades to people out of state. The men will be sentenced in April.

TENNESSEE: *Maybe he was hiding something...* It has been reported that Memphis jailers grew suspicious of a lump in the pants of Freddrick Johnson, 30, an inmate they were processing on a trespassing charge. Mr. Johnson claimed that the bulge was his genitalia, officials said. However, when they threatened with a strip search, he handed over a 2.5-foot machete he had hidden under a rill of his belly flesh.

TENNESSEE: *The headline read, Worst. Date. Ever.* Kelton Griffin of Memphis is accused of stealing his date's car – and using it to take another woman out to see a movie. On top of that after the two-timing thief was arrested at the Summer Drive-In, the first woman said the second date was her god sister.

WEST VIRGINIA: *BAD BAIT!* It has been reported that two men fell for a trap set by police when they allegedly tried to steal Christmas packages from a front porch. The men did not know that the packages were empty inside, except for a note that read, "Merry Christmas. Wheeling Police Department." Scott Ruttencutter, 37 and Casey Higgs, 29, were arrested on charges of theft.

CHAPTER 4

Lots of Stories From The Sunshine State

Professor Birdsong's 157 Dumbest Thieves

FLORIDA: *Shell Shocker?* A police officer pulled over a truck in the town of Punta Gorda, for rolling through a stop sign and ended up finding 41 small turtles in the backpack of passenger Ariel LeQuire, police said. When asked whether she had anything else on her person, Ms. LeQuire pulled a 1-foot long alligator from her yoga pants. Police report that she and the driver were cited for possession of protected species.

FLORIDA: *Idiot fugitive?* A fugitive tried to outsmart police by leaving a note on a mattress that said he wasn't home. "I know my warrant is active," said the note at Jesse Pack's Bunnell residence. "I'm not here. I'm finishing a job and turning myself into the Volusia Branch of jail." We learn that the police being unconvinced searched the bedroom, and reportedly found Pack, 40, wanted on kidnapping and aggravated-assault charges – in a bedroom dresser. Off to jail he went.

FLORIDA: *Someone really digs money...* Pembroke Pines public-works employees were in for a surprise in late January 2019, when they showed up to deal with a "sinkhole" – and found it was part of a tunnel dug from a nearby wooded area to a Chase bank branch, presumably as part of a heist plot. It has been reported that the FBI is investigating.

FLORIDA: *A crappy surprise!* A man was arrested for stealing painkillers that turned out to be laxatives, police report. Peter Emery, 56, of Pinellas Park, allegedly snatched the drug from a locked box inside the victim's home. The pill bottle was labeled "hydrocodone acetaminophen" but was actually filled with Equate Gentle laxatives.

FLORIDA: *IDIOT!* A bandit was foiled by his own John Hancock – when he signed for a package at the house he was burglarizing, and soon was arrested. Travis Thompson, 34, took a break from ransacking the home in Key West to brainlessly sign his real name after the deliveryman asked for his signature, according to police.

FLORIDA: *Naked cash?* During the end of January 2018, an alleged bank robber who stripped down to his birthday suit and ran through the streets throwing stolen cash in the air went on trial. We learn that it took only 25 minutes of testimony for the judge to find Alexander Sperber, 26, whose naked flight from a Region's Bank in Fort Lauderdale was captured on cell-phone video, not guilty by reason of insanity.

FLORIDA: *Too much meat in his pants?* An Indiantown man was apprehended stealing from a grocery store after a police officer observed him pulling a full rack of ribs from the waistband of his trousers, according to police authorities. Maeli Alverez, 26, was also caught swiping two packages of hamburger buns, nine pieces of fried chicken, and mashed potatoes at the Rines Market IGA in Indiantown. Yes, an arrest was made.

FLORIDA: *Irony, maybe?* The Superintendent of Schools in Melbourne almost got a ticket. Desmond Blackburn was driving his official SUV in early April 2018 when he illegally passed a stopped school bus where students were disembarking while local police were running a bus-safety campaign, called "Operation BUSted." The embarrassed superintendent did not receive a ticket but was sent on his way after being given a warning by bemused officers.

FLORIDA: *Backstreet Boy – NOT!* A man was finally arrested after years of allegedly using celebrities' names on fake checks. Michael Watters, 48, was charged with 22 counts of identity fraud for writing and cashing checks using the names of Backstreet Boy Howard "Howie D." Dorough and MLB players Johnny Damon and Sterling Hitchcock, authorities said.

FLORIDA: *The headline read, "Her home was invaded by a bare."* We learn that a naked man ransacked a 93-year-old woman's house, leaving behind a candy wrapper and chocolate smudges. The Edgewater woman awoke to find Shawn Plotts in her home, police said. He allegedly scattered her belongings before fleeing. Police discovered Plotts wandering outside in jeans, with the woman's drivers' license, credit car and car keys.

FLORIDA: *Crime stopping?* It has been reported that a would-be robber was arrested before he ever set foot inside a bank. Why? Because he was wearing a heavy flannel shirt and a ski mask on a 90-degree day. Tellers at the Hollywood, Wells Fargo bank saw 46-year-old David Licht ambling up to the door dressed like a robber from central casting on a Saturday in mid-July, so they locked the branch and called 911. Authorities charged him with attempted bank robbery.

FLORIDA: *They say this man's 20-minute airport visit was plane nuts.* Drew Bronnenburg, 28, after getting into a fight with his girlfriend, is accused of stripping down to his boxers and hopping the fence at Tampa's O. Knight Airport. Once there, he allegedly tried to steal two planes (he did not know how to start them) and drove around in a golf cart and an airport fuel truck before crashing into a building and being charged with burglary, criminal mischief and grand theft.

FLORIDA: *Caught red-handed*? A crook was caught trying to steal money from a church donation box. Charles Hinckley, 34, got his arm stuck in the box at the Trinity Episcopal Church in Vero Beach and began bleeding when he tried to free himself, authorities said. Hinckley was arrested after police freed his arm.

FLORIDA: *The headline read, "What a saucy love triangle."* Two men, John Silva and Derrick Irving, stand accused of breaking into their former lover's house and trying to burn it down using a can of spaghetti sauce. It was reported that Irving was wearing a bull costume. The two burglars then stole electronics from their former boyfriend's house. Police found a can of spaghetti sauce left on a stove burner, as well as a washcloth place near the open flame.

FLORIDA: *You snooze, you lose!* A woman broke into a vehicle at a car dealership near Ocala to take a nap and accidently lit the car on fire with a lit cigarette, according to a police report. Dolores Graham, 62, was arrested for burglary.

FLORIDA: *Birdnapping?* In mid-March a thief was chased by a flock of peacocks when he snatched one of birds from the flock from outside of a Miami home. The thief, caught on surveillance-camera was able to reach his truck and escaped before being assaulted by the flock, authorities said. No arrest has been made.

FLORIDA: *Naked robot?* It has been reported that a thief snatched the clothes off a retired robot at Disney World. The bandit sneaked into a backstage area of the Orlando theme park and peeled a jacket and cap off of Buzzy, a plastic automaton once featured in the "Wonders of life" attraction at Epcot. The robot clothes were valued at $600, police report. No arrest has been made.

FLORIDA: *A very special hiding place, no?* A thief allegedly hid four Rolex watches in a very special spot – her privates. Delajurea Brookens, 29, was charged with stealing the watches valued at $108,000 from a business man she met at a Miami Beach Club. Police who caught her holding one watch, allegedly found the others during a jailhouse strip-search.

FLORIDA: *Prince Fraudster!* It has been reported that Anthony Gignac did a great job posing as a Saudi prince interested in investing hundreds of millions of dollars in Miami Beach's iconic Fontainebleau hotel, according to a police report. However, the hotel owner, after giving Gignac $50,000 in gifts, became very suspicious when the Muslim prince wolfed down pork and bacon at a breakfast meeting. Gignac is now facing multiple fraud charges.

FLORIDA: *The headline read, "Birdbrained break-in bust."* This was the case of the stolen chicken dinner at a police station. Police in Boynton Beach were arriving for a morning shift when they found a broken window and the remains of a hastily eaten meal in the kitchen. Yvlande Jean-Pierre, 29, left behind her wallet which contained two identification cards, police said. Security video allegedly shows she spent 45 minutes in the police station substation before leaving. Ms. Jean-Pierre has been arrested and charged with burglary.

FLORIDA: *Yep, she picked the wrong guy to scam.* It has been reported that a greedy clerk allegedly tried to steal winning lottery-ticket prize money, however, she picked the wrong person to scam. The man was actually an undercover Florida Lottery Commission agent, hired to keep clerks honest. Winn-Dixie Liquors worker Crystelle Baton, 42 of Fort Myers, told the agent that his $600 winning ticket was worth only $5.00, according to authorities. She allegedly slid the winning ticket into a notebook and was arrested on the spot.

FLORIDA: *11-year-old arrested at school?* An 11-year-old boy was arrested in February 2019, after refusing to stand for the Pledge of Allegiance and arguing with the substitute teacher, contending, "The flag is racist and the national anthem is offensive to black people." The boy was a sixth grader at a middle school in Lakeland. A school in Polk County. He received a three-day suspension for disrupting a school function. The law in Florida does not make not standing for the Pledge of Allegiance a crime. The substitute teacher did know this, and we learn from a spokesman for the school that the substitute will not be returning to Polk County schools

FLORIDA: *Did him dirty?* We learn that Matt Crull, 29, is being freed after spending 41 days in jail for allegedly possessing heroin -- that was really laundry detergent, authorities say. The Martin County Sheriff's deputy who arrested Crull and at least 11 other innocent people were fired.

FLORIDA: *The return of "Shoeless Joe."* A man who allegedly broke into a Brevard County home was arrested after he left one of his shoes at the scene of the crime, according to police. Joseph Knight, 27 allegedly stole guns, a PlayStation, a projector, a wall safe, and $300, but left one of his shoes in the getaway car, caught on video surveillance. The Toyota Corolla was owned by Knight's mother's boyfriend, who identified Knight in the video from the crime scene.

FLORIDA: *Were those wienies good enough to die for?* A man swiped $10 worth of frankfurters from a grocery store and then jumped off a bridge to escape police. David Bertram, 41, was being escorted to a police car after officers caught him stealing the hot dogs in Fort Walton Beach when he darted away from his captors and then ran through highway traffic to leap off an 8-foot bridge. Police report he was again caught, Tasered, arrested and charged.

FLORIDA: *They called it a "penny-ante" crime.* A woman who got so mad at a 7-Eleven store clerk because he refused to accept payment in pennies that she pulled a handgun and fled. Adekemi Ayeni, 20, allegedly flipped out after the clerk in the town of Melbourne said he didn't have room in his register for her coins.

FLORIDA: *Bad houseguest?* A friend visiting the home of a retired deputy sheriff swiped an old uniform and tried to persuade pharmacy workers to give him drugs, according to a police report. It appears that Johnny Wilson dressed up in the green uniform and gesturing to his badge, allegedly demanded pain pills from a Pensacola pharmacist. When she refused, he snatched a pair of pants and a soda and ran from the store without paying.

FLORIDA: *It's all over for one alleged toll beater.* Joshua Concepcion-West was recently arrested when police say they caught him using a remote-controlled gadget that lowered a curtain over his license plate before he drove through an Orlando toll booth and raised the curtain once he got to the other side.

FLORIDA: *IDIOT!* A wanna-be burglar picked the worst place in the world for a break-in – a surveillance camera shop. The hood was caught on several hidden cameras trying to smash in a door at Spy Spot Investigations in Deerfield Beach, police report.

FLORIDA: *An arrest of a biting shoplifter.* We learn from a police report that Darrien Giannelli, 23, was trying to steal $110 worth meat from a Boynton Beach Publix supermarket when a 65-year-old good Samaritan intervened to stop the theft and was bitten by Giannelli for his trouble. Police were called and Giannelli was arrested.

FLORIDA: *Yet, another biting incident!* A chubby thief tried to steal lingerie from a Victoria's Secret in Florida; police were called and apprehended the thief who then bit an officer's thumb. As three officers struggled to handcuff Algernon Baker, who was suspected of shoplifting $750 worth of ladies' undies, he chomped down in a futile bid to flee. We learn he is out of jail on bond awaiting trial for grand theft and assault on a peace officer.

FLORIDA: *OOPS...Could this have been a "joint investment?"* A woman bought a used couch online and discovered it was stuffed with marijuana. The woman realized that something was up when the seller began frantically texting her, contending she had left something important in one of the cushions. "You're stealing from me!" the seller texted, insisting she return the pot. Instead, the buyer called the police.

Professor Birdsong's 157 Dumbest Thieves

CHAPTER 5

Thieves From The Good Old Midwest

Professor Birdsong's 157 Dumbest Thieves

MINNESOTA: *Those Must Have Been Some Really Big Pants!* A suburban Minneapolis man managed to walk out of a store with a 19-inch TV shoved down his pants. He also had a remote control for the TV, power cords and a bottle of brake fluid in his pants. Eric Lee King, 21, was caught when a police officer saw him drop a box of candy in the parking lot. The officer realized that King was walking strangely and at the same time he was trying to hold up his pants.

ILLINOIS: *The headline read, "Bloody sundae."* One summer day a Chicago bandit robbed an ice-cream truck with an assault rifle. It is reported that the thief pulled the weapon, demanded cash and the keys to the truck and fled in the vehicle. No arrest has been made.

INDIANA: *Undies chase?* Police were surprised when they spotted bras and panties flying from a car amid a high-speed chase. The police were trailing Holly Sansone, 34 – who had allegedly shoplifted from a store in Portage – at about 100 mph when the undies started flying. At least four bras and 14 pairs of panties were scattered on the road. Yes, she was arrested.

INDIANA: *Hard pills to swallow.* In June 2018, police seized dozens of bright orange "ecstasy pills shaped like President Trump's head. The image of Trump's face is stamped on the tablets along with the phrase "GREAT AGAIN." Police confiscated the pills in connection with 129 drug-related arrests in northern Indiana.

INDIANA: *Undies chase?* Police were surprised when they spotted bras and panties flying from a car amid a high-speed chase. The police were trailing Holly Sansone, 34 – who had allegedly shoplifted from a store in Portage – at about 100 mph when the undies started flying. At least four bras and 14 pairs of panties were scattered on the road. Yes, she was arrested.

IOWA: *The headline read, "He is the taped crusader."* A sword-wielding bandit was caught on camera robbing a convenience store. The crook allegedly held up Casey's General Store in Council Bluffs with the sword and a rifle. He and his accomplice in a green Spandex onesie fled with cash. No arrest has yet been made.

IOWA: *Maybe he is a monster?* A man named King Kong – really – was arrested recently after allegedly chasing children and threatening to eat them. Witnesses say King Kong Choul mumbled he would put "seasoning" on them and "cut them to pieces." Fortunately, he was charged with harassment.

KANSAS: *The headline read, "He's hot for hot rods."* A drunken man allegedly tried to have "sex" with the tailpipe of a parked car – not once, but twice. Neighbors saw Ryan Malek, 23, allegedly attempting to insert his penis into a vehicle that didn't belong to him near an apartment complex in the town of Newton. Police later saw him pulling the same move – and he was charged with lewd and lascivious behavior.

MICHIGAN: *What a jerk!* There is not much one Michigan man wouldn't do on the first date -- including stealing a car! Terrance Dejuan McCoy, 23, allegedly asked his victim out to dinner, but when the check came, he told his date he had left his wallet in her car. After the trusting woman tossed him the keys, he stuck her with the bill and sped off, police said.

MICHIGAN: *Idiot! Perhaps, he missed the prison food...or the prison sex?* A parolee who robbed a Michigan bank was caught when he tried to hitch a ride from an undercover police detective, police said. Mark White flagged down Saginaw detective Scott Jackson after the bank robbery a few blocks away, say police. White had been paroled 30-days earlier after serving time for a DUI.

MICHIGAN: *Maybe that's why you are in jail dummy...* A Western Michigan University student committed what a judge called "the dumbest crime I've heard" by stealing a computer from the Kalamazoo County jail where he was serving time for another crime. William Bradley, a 25-year-old sophomore admitted, "I'm not the best criminal."

MICHIGAN: *Such a creepy story. Leave the dead alone.* Vincent Bright, 49, pleaded guilty to sneaking into a Detroit graveyard and digging up the body of his late father, Clarence Bright, with the intention of bringing him back to life. Authorities are not sure how Vincent was going to bring his father back to life, but it is reported that he was caught after family members learned of his ghoulish plan.

MICHIGAN: *DUMMY*... A bank robbery suspect was arrested at a Southfield strip club after he allegedly hung red dye coated bills on the strippers' G-strings, and the manager called the police. Sometimes in bank robberies, tellers hand over cash stacks with exploding dye packs that spew ink on the cash and the robber.

MICHIGAN: *Roseville should make their police force "flush out" the thieves...* The town of Roseville is under siege by a bathroom bandit! One or more "crapper crooks" have been breaking into restrooms at gas stations and fast food joints and stealing plumbing fixtures. The thieves steal all of the toilets' flush handles and water pipes, leaving locals high and dry.

MICHIGAN: *Getaway snowmobile?* It has been reported that a man drove a stolen snowmobile straight into a party store in a strange bid to steal cigarettes and lottery tickets. Michael Stark allegedly plowed the vehicle into the store's front door. Police found him in a ditch after following the snowmobile tracks leading away from the scene.

MICHIGAN: *"Ruff ride,"* read the headline. A man was arrested for alleged DWI after an officer spotted him parked in the middle of an intersection – preparing a sandwich for his dog. The pickup driver allegedly made the road-blocking pit stop near the town of Grayling because his dog, Lucky, hungry, authorities said. The doggie downed the snack and was handed over to a relative of its owner, who was soon eating jailhouse food.

MINNESOTA: *Can we say it was a "cool" arrest...?* A man was arrested for allegedly stealing Freon from a neighbor's air conditioner and inhaling the refrigerant. Brentyn Krueger, 36, was found slumped over his neighbor's outdoor air conditioner units, according to the police report.

MINNESOTA: *The headline to this one could have read" "This crime was jug of bull."* A bandit stole $70,000 worth of bull semen from a farm in LeRoy. It appears that a storage unit in the farm's milking parlor was left unlocked, allowing the still at large thief to swipe the valuable material. Perhaps it was an inside job.

MINNESOTA: *Hell, hath no fury like...* When a man rejected Panhia Vang's marriage proposal, she raced off in his Hummer at speeds of 80 mph – with the man clinging to the roof. After he fell off he was rushed to a hospital with multiple broken bones, police said. Vang, allegedly drunk, was charged with car theft and criminal vehicle operation resulting in substantial bodily harm.

MISSOURI: *Hey? Where's the beef?* A thief has been swiping cuts of meat from St. Louis restaurants. We learn that the beef bandit has already hit two area eateries since January 2018, including the Salt+Smoke BBQ twice. At the barbeque restaurant, the bandit stole the meat right out of a smoker. Police describe the man as a 6-foot-tall man in his 40's with a brown mustache and beard.

OHIO: *Stinky?* A man who was charged with criminal mischief for knocking over a porta-potty will now have to scoop up animal poop as part of his punishment. "You act like an animal, you're going to take care of animals," Judge Michael Ciconetti told Bayley Toth. "You want to screw around with crap I will let you do it." Toth was ordered to shovel manure from horses and pigs at the Lake County Fair.

OHIO: *The headline read, "He popped the vault, then he popped the question."* Early this year a man was accused of robbing a bank and using the stolen proceeds to buy his girlfriend an engagement ring. Dustin, Pederson, 36, allegedly stole $8,000 from a Fifth Third Bank in the town of Trenton and then bought a $4,500 ring less than an hour later. He was soon caught and arrested. There is no news concerning the proposed wedding date.

OHIO: *"Best burglars ever,"* read *the headline.* Two strange bandits broke into an Ohio home, washed the owner's clothes and made a pot of coffee – before a relative of the owners caught them in the act. Richard Nippell and Camri Cantwell are also accused of stealing jewelry, a computer and credit cards during their uninvited spree in Uniontown. We learn that the relative of the homeowner held the oddball bandits at gun point until police arrived.

OKLAHOMA: *Sex toy crash & grab?* A burglar crashed his car into the glass doors of a Tulsa adult novelty shop on a Sunday night, then ran inside and stole lingerie and sex toys, police said. The 3 am caper at the Hustler Hollywood store wasn't discovered until employees arrived for work later Monday morning. Authorities believe the thief captured on surveillance video stole items valued between $300 - $400.

WISCONSIN: *Yep, he was a "Bozo."* A county commissioner wore a clown suit to court to argue that his $10 ticket for driving without a seatbelt was a joke. Mark McCune, who serves Washington County, donned clown shoes, makeup and a wig, irking Judge Steven Cain, who said the bozo move was an "insult to the court." McCune had to pay the fine.

WISCONSIN: *Sort of like Robin Hood...except the poor never factored in...* Two robbers loaded down with cash and gems were immediately robbed by a second group of thieves as they walked out the door of a Milwaukee jewelry shop. Police ultimately arrested all four men, but the jewelry and cash were not recovered.

WISCONSIN: *Robbing Peter to Pay Paul?* Police arrested a Wisconsin teen for allegedly breaking into a car and stealing goods so he could get money to pay his lawyer, who was defending him on previous theft charges. Officers found a GPS system, nine CD's and seven video games in the teen's backpack. Actually, he was charged previously with theft, drug possession, and disorderly conduct.

WISCONSIN: *Sounds like girls gone wild.* A naked bid for leniency just did not work. Julia Laack, 36, of Sheboygan was sentenced to six months in jail for shoplifting. When police went to her home, the drunken Laack stripped down to her underwear and told them they couldn't arrest her because she was naked. She eventually pleaded no contest.

WISCONSIN: *This fellow should watch CSI reruns everyday while in the slammer.* Police in La Crosse tracked down a thief who stole a tavern's safe, thanks to DNA collected from the chewing tobacco spit he left behind at the scene of the crime. A fisherman found the empty safe washed up on a sandbar in Illinois.

Professor Birdsong's 157 Dumbest Thieves

CHAPTER 6

Mainly Texas Thieves and Other Cut-Ups

Professor Birdsong's 157 Dumbest Thieves

TEXAS: *Real Life Gangsters?* It has been reported that burglars broke into a house and snatched a machine gun and drank two bottles of Cristal champagne, each bottle costing $300, according to police. Big Springs police are offering a $1,000 reward for the champagne popping bandits who also made off with a home security system.

TEXAS: *He pulled out his manhood and she pulled out her pistol.* A 69-year-old Houston woman said she warned a deranged man pleasuring himself on her porch not to try to enter her home. When he didn't listen, she pulled out her pistol and shot the 38-year-old man in the chest. We learn that the man underwent surgery and is expected to survive.

TEXAS: *Oh, how silly!* Border patrol agents caught smugglers with 3,000 pounds of marijuana – made to look like watermelons. They tried to sneak the weed in on a truck by wrapping the pot in green bundles at the Pharr international Bridge cargo facility, authorities said.

TEXAS: *She was a real pistol.* A hot-tempered lady pointed a gun at another mother over her bad driving skills outside their children's' school. The argument broke out as the parents waited in a drop-off line at Deer Park Elementary School. The children were still in the back seats when one mother pointed a firearm at the other. It has been reported that no one was arrested for this assault.

TEXAS: *The headline read, "They tossed his buns in jail."* A bandit was arrested for robbing a hamburger joint using only a pair of tongs, police said. David Gonzalez was lingering inside a Whataburger in Austin when he allegedly snatched the cooking tool, jabbed an employee with it and demanded cash from the registers. He was soon arrested.

TEXAS: *Yo quiero Taco Bell idiot.* Dallas police arrested a man on Christmas Eve, 2018 after they say he tried to carjack several drivers at gunpoint – demanding that they take him to get tacos. Canamar Garza, 26, allegedly fired multiple rounds hitting one driver in the lower body. Police charged him with aggravated assault and aggravated kidnapping.

TEXAS: *Bumbling Burglars?* Two burglars were recently foiled by their own clumsiness when they tried to ransack a Best Buy store and one of them butt-dialed 911. After an alarm went off, police were headed to the electronics store in Sugar Land when a dispatcher reported a dead-air emergency call nearby. Police pinged the bandits' cellphone near the shop then located their getaway truck and found stolen laptops inside.

ARIZONA: *Wild Child!* It has been reported that a Phoenix-area police officer first tried compassion, responding to a naked woman's claim that she had been a sex-crime victim at a gas station in Gila Bend. However, when the Maricopa Sheriff's deputy went around to the trunk of his cruiser to retrieve a blanket for her, she jumped into the driver' s seat of the car and took off – leading police on a wild 7 ½ mile chase before crashing along I-10 in Elroy, authorities report. She was taken into custody and hospitalized.

MONTANA: *Yes, she sure had a busy day...* It has been reported that Kaylee Berry, 22, of Butte allegedly stole five vehicles – a Dodge Ram, a Pontiac Grand Am, a Ford Ranger, a Toyota Sequoia and a GMC pickup with a dog inside – all in one day. She was charged with five felony counts of theft and one felony count of burglary in the July Sunday 2018 spree.

NEW MEXICO: *Assault with a deadly doughnut?* A man threw a doughnut at a tailgating driver, then allegedly pulled a gun and fired a shot at his foe's car, police report. The suspected road rage gunman Juan Candelaria, 47, was soon arrested by police in Albuquerque.

UTAH: *Meth (od), maybe?* A burglary suspect maintains he couldn't have committed the break-in – because he was high on meth at the time. The St. George man, whose name was not released was being questioned in mid-December 2018 for a burglary when he said he was high on meth that day – and only did break-ins while on heroin. He was arrested anyhow because his fingerprints and shoe prints matched those found at the scene of the crime.

UTAH: *Bang, bang...* An elderly couple put a sign on their Iron Town home that read, "Smith & Wesson spoken here" – and soon proved they meant it. When an alleged burglar, identified as Christian Holbert, 24, entered their home on a Tuesday in August 2018, the couple shot him multiple times, police said. Holbert, reportedly on "some kind of drugs," stripped naked and was tasered by police before taken into custody.

UTAH: *The headline read, "Any way you slice it, that's wrong.* We learn that at least four Salt Lake City parking-compliance officers were fired in December 2017 for allegedly letting restaurant workers park illegally – in exchange for free pizza. An "unusual pattern" of voided tickets near the Sicilia Pizza Kitchen prompted a city probe that reportedly found that workers mostly ducked tickets by displaying Sicilia Pizza menus on the dashboards of their cars.

Professor Birdsong's 157 Dumbest Thieves

CHAPTER 7

Thieves From California & The Pacific Coast

Professor Birdsong's 157 Dumbest Thieves

CALIFORNIA: *Robbers usually put their masks on before the heist – not during it.* Quincy Petty, 39, allegedly walked into the Dollar Tree in Roseville and announced, "Open your register, I'm robbing you," After Petty hinted he had a gun he remembered to put on his mask, police said. Petty was arrested just hours later when an employee identified him as the boyfriend of coworker at the store, according to police.

CALIFORNIA: *The headline read, "He took his meal to go – and police now have beef with him."* A man in a suit was caught on camera wrapping a pricey steak in a cloth napkin at a restaurant and then skipping out on the bill. The bandit took one bite from the 20-ounce porterhouse and looked around nervously inside the House of Beef in Oakdale before sprinting out with the steak.

OREGON: *Yo ho, ho, and a bottle of rum...* A thief wearing a pirate mask was caught on camera robbing a bar. The bandit slipped through a back door at the Last Lap in the town of Cornelius and snatched $4,000 from a safe, the bar owner said. Police are using surveillance footage to track him down. No arrest yet.

OREGON: *Why leave a note?* A Portland woman swiped a package off a porch and left a note behind that read: "Hey! Thank you for the package!" However, the homeowner, Mair Blatt has surveillance equipment that recorded images of the thief, who swiped a $17 bottle of hair oil and then ditched the box. Mr. Blatt is confident that the thief will be caught.

CALIFORNIA: *Double trouble, maybe?* A man allegedly stole two vans from the same mortuary – returning the first after he found a corpse in the back. Bobby Washington, 24, took the first hearse at about 1:30 am on a Sunday February, but returned it when he found the cadaver, Riverside police said. That's when he was arrested while trying to steal the second van, authorities said. Police have not determined his motive for stealing the funeral vans.

OREGON: *The headline read: "Thieves took the roof over a man's head."* A Las Vegas man whose custom built, 95-square-foot house was recently stolen from an east Oregon truck stop got his house back. Lawrence Thomas' tiny home was snatched when he stopped to avoid severe weather as he drove it from Seattle to Las Vegas. The house was found just a half-mile from the site of the theft.

CALIFORNIA: *Bad roommate?* A man swiped his roommate's winning $10 million scratch-off while the roommate slept. He then tried to cash in on the winnings, authorities said. Adul Saosongyang, 35, was arrested when he went to a state lottery office in Sacramento in early 2019 to collect the cash.

CALIFORNIA: *"BUSTED."* We learn that a 45-year-old woman was recently caught smuggling $10,000 worth of black tar heroin from Mexico to California – in her bra. The suspect, a U.S. citizen was crossing the El Centro Sector border in Imperial, when she was singled out by a drug-sniffing dog, authorities said. Must have been a big bra!

OREGON: *A horse is a horse of course of course...* It has been reported that a horse is suing his former owner for negligence after they left him starved, covered with lice and badly frostbitten. Justice, an 8-year-old quarter horse, is named as the plaintiff in a lawsuit filed by his new owners, who are treating him well on a farm in the Cascade mountain range. According to the suit the revenge seeking stud wants $100,000 for veterinarian care along with "pain and suffering."

CALIFORNIA: *Attempted gumball theft.* A clumsy burglar smashed a window at a Front Street Animal Shelter in Sacramento and climbed into the building. He then tried to pull a large gumball machine back out through the window, however it was too large, and the treats spilled onto the floor, a surveillance video shows. The burglar eventually fled without the machine.

CALIFORNIA: *The headline read, "His luck ran out."* A former security guard who won $19 million in the California lottery pleaded guilty to robbing four banks in a string of much-less-lucrative robberies. James Hayes, who hit the jackpot two decades ago, handed notes to several tellers demanding cash, and sometimes claimed to have a gun, during the LA area hold-ups. It appears he made off with a total of $40,000, less than 1 percent of his lottery winnings. We wonder where the lottery money went?

CALIFORNIA: *They deserve each other.* Thieves broke open a mailbox and swiped a package – which was filled with 500 cockroaches. Rosalinda Vizina, an entomologist from Seaside, said the roaches were for a study. "I hope they went everywhere," she said.

CALIFORNIA: *The headline read: "The FBI better call the police."* We learn that a Special FBI agent in Costa County, was the victim of a car theft – and the bandit got away with the agent's submachine gun, ammo magazines and his bulletproof vest. No suspects have been identified.

CALIFORNIA: *The headline read: "No good deed goes unpunished."* Katherine Sasseen put a sign outside her El Cerrito, home inviting people to use her bike for free. When she returned from a walk, a man in her back yard pretended to inquire about her bike. Then he suddenly bolted from the yard, leaving behind her laptop and other electronics under a blanket.

CALIFORNIA: *Sounds more like a crime bus than a party bus!* We learn that robbers held up a 7-Eleven store – and then made their getaway in party bus. The 7-Eleven clerk in Huntington Beach, who was robbed and assaulted advised police that the robbers got away in the bus. Officers later pulled over the bus on the Pacific Coast highway and interviewed the 80 people on board. Two of them were arrested and seven loaded handguns were confiscated, officials report.

CALIFORNIA: *The headline read: "Worst bank robber ever!"* Alvin Lee Neal, 56, was recently sentenced to three years and 10 months in prison for robbing a Wells Fargo bank in San Diego last May. Moments before demanding money, Neal inexplicably swiped his ATM card in a reader at the teller's window, thereby revealing his identity, officials said.

Professor Birdsong's 157 Dumbest Thieves

CHAPTER 8

Stories of Thieves From Abroad

Professor Birdsong's 157 Dumbest Thieves

AUSTRAILIA: *A naked carjacking?* A Brisbane man desperately tried to prevent thieves from stealing his beloved pickup truck by clinging to the back of it wearing nothing but a towel around his waist. Bobby Cook was in the shower when he heard the engine of his Toyota Hilux. Cook ran outside and jumped on the back of it, holding on as the bandits drove for 20 minutes. The carjackers eventually shook off Cook, who suffered a minor head injury.

CANADA: *Sticky situation?* We learn that three bandits stole $20,000 worth of maple syrup and then led police on a high-speed chase. They were subsequently sent to jail. In this most Canadian crime ever, the bandits allegedly swiped the sweet sap from a truck in Alberta and led police on a wild chase.

CHINA: *The headline read, "fowl play."* A Shanghai man was arrested when he stole a black swan from a public park – and cooked it and ate it with a side of radishes. The man, a delivery driver known only as Zhou, 30, was sentenced to six months in jail for his strange taste for water birds. Authorities said he had been fishing with Friends at the park when he snatched the bird that he later cooked and ate at home.

COLOMBIA: *Follow the money?* A Colombian woman swallowed $7,000 in U.S. currency to keep it from her husband in a bitter divorce dispute. In terrible pain, the woman went to Santander University Hospital in Bucaramanga – where doctors removed $5,700 from her stomach. "The dollar notes were washed and are in good condition, but the rest of the money was lost because of the gastric fluids," said a surgeon.

COLOMBIA: *Cheater?* An angry Uber driver caught his wife having an affair when she and her lover unwittingly hired him to drive them to a Barranquilla hotel. The husband, identified by police as Yeimy, brawled with the lover when he showed up in a friend's car his wife hadn't recognized.

GERMANY: *Biggest sex-toy heist in history?* It has recently been reported the thieves took $57,000 in kinky merchandise from a Berlin sex-trade show. Fun Toys London – which set up a booth at the Venus Exhibition – said workers realized they had been ripped off when they discovered that nine boxes of erotic toys had vanished.

GERMANY: *Kliene Dumkopf (Little Dummy).* A young boy pulled off a great heist when he stole a bus – and none of the passengers even noticed the lad was behind the wheel. The 11-year-old troublemaker said he found a key to the privately-owned bus and decided to take it for a joyride in Ingolstadt. No one was injured and the boy was released to his mother.

HONG KONG: *Dash for the cash?* Thousands of dollars fell from the sky, sparking a dash for the cash and a police investigation. A mystery man threw bills into the air from the top of a building in a poor section of the city. He later admitted it was as stunt to promote his crypto-currency company.

INDIA: *Gold Shirt Tycoon Murdered?* A man in India who bought one of the world's most expensive shirts, a shirt made entirely of gold, was beaten to death after a dispute over money. Datta Phuge, 48, who commissioned the six-pound shirt for $250,000 three years ago, was attacked by 12 men in the western city of Pune in July 2016, according to a report. It appears that one attacker invited the millionaire businessman to a birthday party where he was jumped, stoned and stabbed with a farming tool. Allegedly the fatal beating was over cash, police say. It had taken goldsmiths two weeks to build the T-shirt, which was decorated with six crystal buttons and a gold belt. *No, he was not murdered while wearing the golden shirt.*

INDIA: *So, so bogus was this arrest....* Police in India are in a spot of trouble for arresting a man for drinking a cup of tea in a "suspicious" manner. Vijay Patil, 49, was sipping chai at a roadside stall when officers handcuffed him and took him to the police station. A Bombay court quashed the charges, calling them "bewildering" after police claimed the man didn't give a good explanation for his tea drinking habits.

IRELAND: *Great-grandfather thrashes criminal thugs*. It has been reported that this senior citizen fought off three weapon-wielding robbers with his bare hands. The bad boys were hauling hammers and a sawed-off shotgun when they stormed 83-year-old Dennis O'Conner's sports betting center Bar One Racing in Glanmire and demanded cash. Instead of backing down, O'Conner tackled one of the crooks and kicked him in the back, causing them all to flee empty-handed.

JAPAN: *AHH-CHOO*.... Japanese police are investigating reports of a middle-aged man offering two male high school students $9 to sneeze in front of him. It is not clear if the man, who offered the payments at a train station in the city of Hamamatsu, broke any laws. However, police insist the probe is in the interest of "maintaining public safety and order."

MEXICO: *Body recovered*. A man stole a car after seeing the keys dangling in the ignition. However, it turned out to be a hearse with a dead body inside. Police in Tlaquepaque say Annibal Saul, 40, stole the vehicle while it was waiting to transport the corpse of an 80-year-old man from a hospital to a funeral home. They caught him on a highway, and both the car and the body were recovered.

NEW ZEALAND: *He was in a real toe jam, read the headline.* The unidentified 28-year-old was charged in late June with stealing two human toes, from an exhibit of preserved bodies in Auckland. He faces up to seven years in prison. The toes, estimated to be worth $3,815, were returned to the Body Worlds Vital display.

NEW ZEALAND: *There's no crook like an old crook.* An elderly man stole dozens of avocados from a family's tree and then fled on a mobility scooter, according to police. Bert Glazer, of Aukland, said his partner spotted the old man and an accomplice knocking the fruit loose with a 12-foot pole, which police dusted for fingerprints. Last year, thieves swiped more than 200 avocados from the same tree.

NEW ZEALAND: *They swiped the whole thing!* A thief took burglary to a new level when he swiped a couple's entire tiny house. Bianca Balducci and her partner Stephen had nearly completed building the insulated 24-by-8-foot white abode in Auckland when the bandit rolled away with it on a trailer bed truck.

SOUTH AFRICA: *The headline read: "Good they weren't stealing watermelons."* We learn that police are in trouble after videos emerged of them catching apple thieves and then pelting the suspects with the stolen fruit. Western Cape officials are investigating the potential misconduct. *OUCH!*

UNITED KINGDOM: *Flatulence city, maybe?* A thief stole 6,000 cans of baked beans from a food delivery truck in England. The bandit struck when the driver fell asleep and he is still at large. Beans, beans, good for the heart, the more you eat the more you…

UNITED KINGDOM: *Is his name Dale the whale?* A morbidly obese Scottish man who used a stolen credit card to purchase $250 worth of pizza failed to appear in court – because he was too obese, his lawyer said. The 21-year-old man, who weighs 550 pounds, pleaded guilty to ordering Domino's four times with the card. Although he pleaded guilty, the judge has put sentencing off to a later date.

UNITED KINGDOM: *The headline read: "Justice for Bessy!"* British police have launched a manhunt for a pervert seen "committing a sexual act" on a cow in Hertfordshire early one Saturday in May. Police are searching by helicopter and asking the public for leads.

UNITED KINGDOM: *THUD!* A Gambian man awaiting deportation in a British detention center was so upset that he wasn't allowed to see his home country's soccer team play on television ran head first into a wall and became paralyzed. We learn that Amadou Nyang is now suing the British government for not stopping from expressing his team loyalty.

UNITED KINGDOM: *They say this theft really hit home.* It appears that the crooks in this heist did not just steal Widow Sonia McColl's belongings – they also loaded her 40-foot mobile home onto a truck and took off with that, too, said police in Cullompton, Devon. "I'm numb," said McColl, 70, who was not home at the time, "They've taken everything I've got."

UNITED KINGDOM: *They said her costume was the bomb!* A British woman dressed as an ISIS recruit at a costume party, then tossed her faux-suicide vest in a trash can, sparking a bomb scare. Police sealed off several streets in Wellingborough, Northamptonshire, and conducted a controlled explosion – only to discover the prop was made of plastic and fake wires.

CHAPTER 9

A Few Miscellaneous Thefts

from Around The U.S.

ALASKA: *Police called him a clumsy "Cat(erpillar) burglar."* An Anchorage man was charged in the theft of a front-end loader that he then allegedly used – as his getaway vehicle. Authorities say Brian Petross, 42, also used the loader to break the front window of a saloon so he could run inside and steal things. He then tried to use the loader in another burglary, but he got caught and was arrested.

ALASKA: *Cardboard box headed thief?* Authorities report that a man in Anchorage has been robbing businesses at knifepoint – with a cardboard box on his head. The bandit robbed two liquor stores and a filling station last week. "Some goofball wearing a cardboard box with two eye hole punched out came in threatened her," said Kevin Wright, whose girlfriend was working at the gas station at the time.

ALASKA: *The headline read, "The robbery suspect was caught cold.* We learn that a 34-year-old man who robbed a Taco Bell in Anchorage tried to evade police by burying his black coat in the snow nearby. However, police officers who found the coat simply followed the tracks in the snow until they found the suspect, by then shivering in the cold temperature.

MARYLAND: *KA-BOOM?* A recent Baltimore gun buyback event took in more than 1,000 firearms – and a rocket launcher. Police are trying to track the origins of the weapon, which was traded in for $500.

MARYLAND: *Idiot white-nationalist Coast Guard Lieutenant!* We learn that the lieutenant with a small arsenal allegedly planned to kill journalists and Democrat party leaders, including Sen Chuck Schumer, House speaker Nancy Pelosi, and Rep. Alexandria Ocasio-Cortez, as well as media personal including CNN and MSNBC's Joe Scarborough, Van Jones and Chris Cuomo. He was arrested in late February 2019, because he used his government computer to compile the hit list. His name is Christopher Hasson, 49, and is now in jail. Prosecutors say Hasson who also served in the Marine Corps and the Army National Guard has long-held extremist neo-Nazi and racist views.

THE END

About the Author

Professor Birdsong received his J.D. from the Harvard Law School and his B.A. from Howard University. He teaches law in Orlando, Florida.

After graduation from law school he worked four years at the law firm of Baker Hostetler. He then entered into a varied and distinguished career in government service. He served as a diplomat with the U.S. State Department with various postings in Nigeria, Germany and the Bahamas.

Professor Birdsong later served as a federal prosecutor. After leaving government service, and before he began teaching, Professor Birdsong was in private law practice in Washington, D.C.

www.BirdsongLaw.com

lbirdsong22@gmail.com

Professor Birdsong's 157 Dumbest Thieves

Ordering Information

New books coming soon!

Dear Reader,

If you liked this book, I would greatly appreciate you writing me a review on Amazon or any other book site.

I look forward to sharing more funny stories with you in future books.

Thank you, I really appreciate your help.

Regards,

Professor Birdsong

Winghurst Publications
1969 S. Alafaya Trail / Suite 303
Orlando, FL 32828-8732
www.BirdsongLaw.com
lbirdsong22@gmail.com

Books by
Professor Birdsong:

- Professor Birdsong's 77 Dumbest Criminals Stories (Kindle & Paperback)

- Professor Birdsong's 147 Dumbest Criminal Stories: Florida (Kindle)

- Professor Birdsong's 157 Dumbest Criminal Stories (Kindle & Paperback)

- Professor Birdsong's Weird Criminal Law Stories (Kindle)

- Professor Birdsong's "365" Weird Criminal Law Stories for Every Day of the Year (Kindle)

- Professor Birdsong's Weird Criminal Law Stories, Volume 2: Stories From Around the States and Abroad (Kindle)

- Professor Birdsong's Weird Criminal Law Stories, Volume 3: Stories From New York City and the East Coast. (Kindle)

- Professor Birdsong's Weird Criminal Law Stories - Volume 4: Stories from the Midwest (Kindle)

- Professor Birdsong's Weird Criminal Law Stories, Volume 5: Stories from Way Out West (Kindle)

- Professor Birdsong's Weird Criminal Law Stories - Volume 6: Women in Trouble (Kindle)

- Professor Birdsong's Weird Criminal Law - Volume 6: Women in Trouble! (Paperback)

- Professor Birdsong's LAW SCHOOL GUIDE: Techniques for Choosing and Applying to Law School

- Professor Birdsong's: IMMIGRATION: Obama must act now!

This page blank per printer requirement.